The Intelligence of Love

The Author

The Intelligence of Love

MANIFESTING YOUR BEING IN THIS WORLD

JOHN DE RUITER

MOBIUS BOOKS

The Publisher: Mobius Books

Library and Archives Canada Cataloguing in Publication
De Ruiter, John, 1959–, author
The intelligence of love : manifesting your being in this world / John de Ruiter.

Issued in print and electronic formats.
ISBN 978-0-9948820-0-4 (paperback).—ISBN 978-0-9948820-1-1 (epub)

1. Self-actualization (Psychology). I. Title.

BF637.S4D458 2015   158.1   C2015-906425-2
C2015-906426-0

Cover Image and Design: Jens Gaethje
Author Photos: Courtesy of The College of Integrated Philosophy

Edited by Nicolas de Ruiter and
the team at The College of Integrated Philosophy

Produced with the assistance of the Government of Alberta, Alberta Media Fund.

Alberta
Government

PC: 34

Contents

All of the learning, all of the books,
all of the teachings, have value only to honesty.
Honesty finds truth in everything.
The only question is, do you know it to the core,
or not?

Preface

What if the answers to life's deepest questions were right in front of you, and all you had to do was open your eyes in a new way? *The Intelligence of Love* invites you to see the truth that is already within you.

"Through profound honesty, we can consciously manifest the depths of what we are," says John. And it begins with the heart. These depths comprise your being, and through your heart, they infuse your life and this world with meaning. Profound honesty means that you are responsible for every movement of your own consciousness, as you live by the clearest voice you know is true within. When you rest there, in openness and softness of heart, depths of truth and love reveal themselves to you.

The Intelligence of Love offers first steps into the depths of truth within you. While John inspires others primarily through meeting and speaking, the teachings presented here illuminate the levels within you that you have always known and longed to enter. There you are face to face with the purity within your own heart, and the potential from that place is endless. John describes how living from your heart mends and enriches all aspects of life, from parenting and relationship, to sexuality, and our place on this planet.

An Awakening Becomes a Calling

AN INTRODUCTION TO JOHN

Since 1986 John de Ruiter has been speaking about truth to people who find profound rest and awakening in his presence and teachings. In meetings, John opens doorways for consciousness, to levels of deeper meaning that he first experienced at the age of 17. He describes his experience as an immersion into an ultimate reality, suddenly lost, and regained when John let go of all attachment:

I stumbled onto being awakened to something that was profoundly amazing, wonderfully life-giving, without understanding the source of it. I wasn't looking for it. I never related to anything like that being in existence; then all of a sudden there was a flowering inside that made everything in this existence pale in comparison. That flowering, that awakening inside, opened up my awareness to everything in existence to be something more beautiful than I had ever seen before. That lasted about a year, and then suddenly, it was gone. In the same way that I couldn't comprehend how it began, I also couldn't comprehend how it ended, or why. Once awakened, it seemed to me inconceivable that it should ever go away.

Once it left, I was profoundly disturbed because I knew I had been connected to something that made the whole universe live, and that without being connected to that, I knew nothing was worth living for. I committed myself to spending my existence in looking for that reality, not knowing what to look for, although I knew the flavour of it, knew what it was like when alive.

After about two years, there was nothing more that I could turn inside out, nothing else to peel and make raw, nothing left but a state of what seemed to me to be never-ending pain. All I knew to do was rest in that deep, in that darkness, in that pain, letting go of ever needing to find that reality I had so wonderfully tasted and lost. Then, to my total surprise, I was astonished when that same reality flowered again in the midst of the rawness and the darkness where I had made my home. I surrendered to it unconditionally, understanding that it does not need to bless me, that I'll give my life to it and it doesn't have to give anything back. I would exist for that reality.

The text is adapted from dialogues between John and questioners in Canada, the United States, Europe, Israel, India, and Australia, from the years 1999 to 2015.

A Brief Glossary

The following terms offered will not completely capture the full reality of consciousness. However, they are reference points for awakening, as well as thousands of meetings. The value of the words is in the truth they reveal in you.

John describes the human being as a network with successive levels of form, with the outermost conditioned by the world, and the innermost meeting the eternal, as follows:

The person is you interacting with those around you, your behavior as a personality.

The self is your conditioned identity, your immediate inner experience. The self is where ego has most play because everything in life seems to revolve around it. While the self tends to distract from what is deeper, it is innocent. Released of their need for positive experience, the self and person become available to expression of what is deeper, the heart and the being.

The body is also a vehicle for truth, attuned to what you are being in your heart. The body adapts to whatever you are being in it, but the natural way of your body is that of the heart, open and soft. In the most quiet way, the body, on its own, reminds you to rest and open your heart.

The heart holds the power of belief, the power to harden and live for the self, or the power to believe a quieter, deeper truth. The heart gives belief to the deep and brings the deep into the self and the person. The nature of the heart is to be open and soft, and when you are in your heart, you heal the distortion of self-oriented patterning. Your heart is the threshold of your being.

You are awareness, choosing to be either honest or dishonest on any level. You can be a quality of being— resistance, okayness, softness, sweetness. You can choose to be in your heart or to close to the deep and live for the self. You, as awareness can go deeper and deeper, and relate to the levels of your being.

Your being is the interface between the eternal dimensions and the physical plane of this world; it is your true and perfect form, a love available but never insistent. Dishonesty in awareness distances you from your being, and therefore the levels of meaning that exist within and beyond your being. As you reside in your heart and respond to your being, the qualities of your being—love and goodness—move into your self. This is how you and this world can be transformed by love.

Knowing is the relationship between consciousness and meaning, whether it is knowing to be kind or knowing a holiness in nature. Knowing is how honesty sees and your heart receives goodness.

Meaning is fundamental to existence, from the absolute to everyday experience. It is what we all want, but we strive to fill ourselves with it, instead of giving ourselves to it. Simply resting and being honest within, meaning moves from the deep into life, as the essence of beauty.

Love at the deepest level is the very movement of meaning and your being. Love is the innermost of everything and the reason for this book.

CHAPTER 1

Awakening to Your Interior

Openness and softness of heart is the door to everything true within. There, in your being, are levels and levels of you, all streaming.

People live looking for meaning outside of themselves. We see because meaning within recognizes meaning without, but we too easily become trapped in the experience of meaning externally instead of going deeper within. We hold onto meaning for ourselves, while our selves are merely our outer forms, a network of memories, desires, and fears. The levels of the self are woven with the patterning and structures of this world. They provide experience, while the purpose of the self is to express your eternal and true form in this life—your being. The self offers expression to the being within, but not entrance into it.

In meetings I show others dimensions within greater than the world without. There is far more within us than we perceive of the universe, our planet, our lives. Within our interiors are myriad levels of form, like the world outside of ourselves, with systems, structures and relationships. You can let these deeper streams into your heart, changing you from the inside out. When we move with authenticity as awareness, that movement isn't going to be as thought and feeling; it is the movement of the being, and that movement is love.

As the heart opens, your being comes into it, and the slightest movement of your own being is as nurturing as holding a baby. The baby sees you, and there's something magical taking place. In the most delicate way, you're known and taken by a depth of recognition that has nothing to do with your conditioned self. What's moving is not a baby-being, but a fullness of being. The baby is just the surface form through which the fullness of being flows. When we relax within, we are like a baby held by our own beings. The more we open and soften, the more interactivity there is between awareness and the being, like a baby responding without understanding.

When awareness becomes quiet and honest, it knows to open and soften, as when you fall asleep each night, awareness returns to openness. The beauty of waking consciousness is to enter your being by choice, which is honesty. Honesty contains its own levels. For example, you can be honest about your emotions, candidly expressing how you feel, but your honesty can go deeper, to the level of your heart. There, your feelings lose value in comparison to the purity of openness and softness.

When you close and harden, you shield your inner vulnerability. You preserve your personal control, but you then forget your true control, which is honesty. Your first power is the most tender weakness in your heart, which relates only to goodness. Openness and softness of heart is the door to everything true within, and your cosmic plug-in. Openness and softness manifests goodness on every level, and allows you to remake yourself by your own being. Through profound honesty, we can consciously manifest the depths of what we are. The infinite responds to the human, and human consciousness evolves. Our true evolution is more than grace. It is the intelligence of love.

We are here for just a little time, long enough in the midst of continual measures of difficulty, to know, to realize, to be, to become and to leave.

This Life is Golden

LIFE IS A GOLDEN OPPORTUNITY TO
MANIFEST LOVE IN ALL YOUR FORMS

Life comes with the immeasurable opportunity for what you really are to become physical. It offers pure awareness the possibility of evolving with great speed, because in every little way that awareness manifests in life, the forms of your self and person offer continuous feedback. Awareness is in constant realization, realizing what it is through its own reflections.

A lifetime in a body offers pure awareness the amount of evolution that might otherwise take tens of thousands of years. The value of this life is golden, an opportunity to manifest love with all the potential of physical form.

When your body dies the opportunity is over, and how you evolved, or not, is in the next. This life is not something to avoid. The meaning of pure awareness being in this life is immeasurable. If you could see it for what it really is, your response to the opportunity would take your breath away. The magnitude of it would be devastating. Take in what you are able to see now. You would be like a mother holding her newborn baby. As soon as she has her baby, she holds it, and she meets with what is there. A meaning and value beyond anything she has known comes into her, and she loves.

Your being, brought out into your life,
provides the meaning of your life.

The Jewel of Consciousness

PURITY OF HEART IS WHERE SEEING AND SURRENDER ARE ONE

You may awaken, but that doesn't mean you surrender to what you see. Awakening is the privilege of awareness to meet reality, but the full purpose of awakening is purity of heart, where awareness gives itself to the truth it sees. You could be blind within but be given to what you do actually know is true, and you would have purity of heart. That is worth more than any awakening. Purity of heart is the jewel of consciousness.

In purity of heart, whatever little bit you know is true, without resistance, you enter. Purity of heart is where knowing, seeing and surrender are one. Whether at its most advanced or most basic form, awareness is equal in the realm of the heart, where purity is in unhindered response to truth. In that way, a simple farmer, or a child, or an impoverished drifter can be as rich as the most sophisticated being. For consciousness, purity of heart is the greatest treasure, and dearly earned.

Many awaken, but few are truly clean as awareness. In consciousness, beauty and cleanness are inseparable. Wherever there is cleanness, there is loveliness. Awakening means that there is new possibility, but only total surrender is in actual realization of that possibility, and this is as real on subtle inner levels as in everyday life.

Within your chest, you may experience a closing of anger, guilt, or denial. Somewhere in that tightening is something to be seen. The moment you soften, even slightly, a truth appears. If there is purity of heart, the moment you see that truth, no matter how it feels, you dive into it. On a more basic level, when you're in the tension of disagreement with somebody you love, the conflict seems too strong and all your sense of rightness is upon you. All of your nervous system is wired by your sense of rightness. For a moment you will catch a glimpse of weakness, in which your entire stance is mistaken. Within that recognition are levels and levels of weakness. When you have purity of heart, you move straight into that weakness, and do everything you can to make right your relationship with the other. You can rest in the full reality of your mistakes, the fullness of your weakness. When you enter that weakness with all of your heart, your heart is pure. You are home and you are complete.

Resting In What You Really Are

WHEN YOU ARE QUIETED WITHIN,
PROFOUND OKAYNESS HAS YOU IN AWE

What you are able to be is a very delicate quality, instead of a person. When you identify such a quality and embody it in your person, it enriches your person and your life. Profound okayness is a quality of being. You were that quality before you discovered your own person. So tender and natural, profound okayness goes unnoticed, but when you are quieted within, profound okayness has you in awe. It's like the most tender exhale, bringing you to softly inhale.

Begin with the moments when your person is at peace. Be that okayness without your person, and then like the tender inhale, bring it back into your person. You are so accustomed to your person that you forget that softness is what you are before you are even aware as a person. Once you experience that delicateness, there is no need to hold the experience. The truth of the quality is in its essence, not your experience of it. Being that quality, without being identified with your person, will turn you into a person of that quality.

Your practical world has your attention, but what is it that gives your practical world value? It is a quality of being you know within. Give your heart to that quality. Your practical world won't suffer. It will be tenderly energized. Your person knows its place as soon as you relate to delicateness. It is as natural as falling asleep when you lie down. You recede into a quality of being and you don't take your physical form with you. You're setting nothing aside, just relaxing into what precedes everything, awareness receding into an essence of love. As easy as that is, you can do the same while awake, but you won't have the same life any more. It will be infused with profound meaning. You are able not only to be that quality, but also to be delighted in it. That is not just profound okayness—that is profound joy.

Your greatest strength is the most delicate touch of being within. Your greatest strength within is in your weakest weakness.

Raising Your Self Like Your Child

YOUR GROWTH WITHIN IS INFORMED
ONLY BY WHAT YOU KNOW THE TRUTH OF
IN YOUR HEART

Questioner: I feel disconnected from my daughter and I don't know how to say no to her.
John: The openness you know in this connection is how you can lead your child into what is deeper than her self. Say yes as openness and say no as softness. When you say no to her as this, you meet with her and she is loved. She's seen and she's known. That much alone exceeds the best parenting.

Questioner: How do I anchor in this?

John: Without using your patterned self to do so. Then she'll see in you how she also doesn't need to use her self to anchor within. She will see that meaning matters more to you than your own self, and she will love it. She'll grow up witnessing an orientation that she knows the truth of. You'll be giving her no reason to be lost. When knowing means more to you than seeing, and seeing means more to you than experiencing, she'll be realizing what she is, easily and quickly. She'll be growing up in it.

Questioner: I doubt that I am capable of this.

John: Has doubt ever informed you of what you do know? Don't listen to your familiar self concerning what you do know in your heart. You'll be growing in a way that isn't informed by your past. The growing within is informed only by what you know the truth of in your heart, however little that is. That allows your self to rest. Your self then no longer has to produce for you what you've been requiring of it. What you're requiring of your self is beyond its scope.

Your self isn't able to produce for you what you are, but you are able to produce in your self what you are. That makes you, awareness, the provider for your self, leaving your self unburdened. Let your self rest concerning everything that is deeper than what your self is. You are more than your self and your self rests in that, and there your daughter can rest as well. She will be growing up in it, receiving the same meaning that your deeper levels provide for your self. Raise your child like you raise your self.

When you are littler, finer, softer than your self,
you are more than the sum of your experiences,
enabling you to guide your self into goodness.

CHAPTER 2

Living from the Heart

No longer relying on your self for meaning, nor seeking satisfaction for yourself, you enter a whole world of goodness within. This is the domain of your heart, which holds nothing for itself and embraces life with a child's purity. In the heart, offense is received but not taken; difficulty is an opportunity to open and evolve as awareness. Everything that comes your way brings more of the deep into your life. The heart is a well, drawing in your being. Pain and confrontation, brought into the heart, draw more and more of your being, which is love.

When you rest in the weakness of your own heart,
your being moves and your self becomes quieted.
In that quiet is the beginning of awakening.

Heart Nectar

WITH NECTAR IN YOUR MIND INSTEAD OF THINKING, YOU HAVE UNDERSTANDING AND WISDOM

Your mind can recall what you know, but your heart knows on its own. Your mind knows when your mind and your heart are one, but serving yourself, the mind only thinks. When the heart is filled with knowing, the heart becomes the seat of nectar. The nectar flows through your mind, and fills the mind with heart. With nectar in your mind instead of thinking, you have understanding and wisdom.

When the nectar moves through your emotions, you experience it washing you. Instead of seeing through what you have learned or experienced in the past, you see as goodness sees. It is like having love eyes in the mind. An eternal goodness is moving through your heart, through your body, through your mind, but the heart isn't the source. Your being is coming into your life. Your heart isn't the source of this goodness; it is where you let the goodness flow.

Notice the Little

IT IS ONLY WHEN YOU ARE BEING IN YOUR
HEART THAT YOU CAN SEE WHAT YOU KNOW

You are used to noticing what is large in your mind.
You overlook the tender little. It is that which touches
your heart and connects you with meaning. Enjoy sipping
a cappuccino and then notice what is happening within.
Notice what is magical and remain in that. That gives
you new eyes, and you will see what it is that you are
being. You will see it all around you. You will recognize
that it has always been there. It is only you that has been
gone, not it, gone somewhere in your mind, instead of
being in your heart.

It is only when you are being in your heart that you
can see what you know. When you are being in your
heart, seeing what you know, you let all of your heart
dissolve into what you know. That is you returning to the
source. That is you being where you came from. That is
you being what it is that you are most deeply longing for,
being it instead of looking for it.

When you look in your mind for what you know, all you
will find is thinking. When you return to where your mind

came from, that is you returning to your heart. Then let yourself return to where your heart came from, which is something that your mind doesn't know. But when you are being in your heart, your heart does know. And when you are surrendering to what your heart knows, you are home.

The Quiet Yes

AS SOON AS YOU'RE QUIETED WITHIN,
SOFTENING IN YOUR HEART MATTERS MORE
THAN ANY ISSUE

The quieter you are as awareness, the more you know. When you are disquieted, your life and issues seem terribly important, but as soon as you're quieted in honesty, softening in your heart matters more. If you're deeply honest within, any awakening brings you to the most quiet, deep, resounding yes. It is goodness to everything in your life. All of this awakening is available to you now. It is yours to enter now, and will be your immersion after you have died. After your physical death, you are pure agreement with all you know. It is only through direct knowledge that you will see, but being in a body allows you to open your inner eyes and find knowledge through honesty.

Every time you lie down to go to sleep, you leave your day and your self behind. You end up entirely in your heart, and just as you fall asleep, you leave behind even that, and you turn to your being. That then informs you how to be with everything in your life.

No matter what is happening in your life, pause, be profoundly honest within, and return to what you know is deeper. From there, your whole life is open to you.

Leading Your Self Into Weakness

IN THE QUIET OF KNOWING,
YOU ANSWER YOUR GREATEST LONGING:
YOUR RETURN TO WHOLENESS

Your thinking leads you into your strength and covers your weaknesses, using your strength to compensate for weakness. For you to come into balance, let go of your strength. Your thinking mind has been used to satisfy and protect your self. Let go of those defenses and enter the weakness. Under the pressure of your life, a shift to weakness is a change in your orientation, from your comforts to what you know in your heart. In holding an orientation to truth, your heart is clean, and your self becomes whole. In weakness, the quiet of knowing, you answer your greatest love and longing, your return to wholeness.

The softer your heart is the less that your past is forming the present and the future.

Receiving Offense

NEGATIVE OUTPOURING IS COMMON
AND HUMAN, BUT ALSO CREATES THE
OPPORTUNITY TO BE WHAT IS UNCOMMON,
AND MOST DEEPLY HUMAN

When somebody affronts you, the energy in your nerves is opening the pathways of your self, and you may either lock in the heat, or allow softness of heart to soothe and reconfigure the network of your self. The offense is an energy. Your little self, unintegrated and full of ego, registers that energy as a chance to experience being right. The little self uses the energy to empower itself. Your nervous system retains the energy and your patterning hardens. Long after the incident is forgotten, the influence holds. Your self is building according to the patterns of reaction, and missing the opportunity to build in meaning.

The energy of reaction is abundantly available. It is the fabric of our ancestry, so embedded that you're harnessing it before you begin to think. The subtleties of your being are most crucial at this moment, so fine, but offering the greatest evolution in that moment of charge. If you take offense, you reaffirm the patterning of your self, favored by the ancestral pattern of reaction. If you gently receive the offense into your heart, your heart grows. When your heart grows, the other is invited into their heart.

Receive injury—openness and softness of heart has endless capacity for it. Your self may still feel inflamed, but your heart is inviting you into what is uncommon in the world, and unfamiliar in your self. Openness and softness of heart is inviting you into your being. If you respond, your being replaces the charge in your nervous system, and your self forms by new pathways, cleared by the streams of your being.

31

When you encounter resistance in your self, you have stumbled upon stolen goods. How lovely! Right there, you can give it all back, and your energy returns to your heart.

All-Weather Love

YOU HAVE DEEPER RESOURCES, AND
DIFFICULTY DRAWS THEM OUT

If you are invested in positive feeling, you're feeding the negative. You exercise the habit of your emotions and that feeds the negative. An emotional habit occupies you and takes up the energy that belongs to what you know in your heart. In the midst of your emotions, identify what you know the truth of in your heart, not what the emotion compels you to believe. Identify a subtlety of goodness. Find what touches your heart and move into it. Then instead of being a habit that lapses into darkness, your emotions will lead you into inner knowledge and equanimity.

As your awareness goes to that, you're exercising what you know. You're developing a subtlety of goodness and you grow; you flourish in the midst of your negative emotion. The emotion passes because it no longer has your attention. If you dance in the sunshine and shrink in the rain, your energy is in the weather. If you dance either way, your energy is in your heart and your happiness has depth without the added difficulty of your preferences. You have deeper resources and difficulty draws them out.

Difficulty is meant to soften your heart. When you resist, you harden your heart, but when you like what you know, you open and you soften. Like what you know in your heart while you're in the midst of unpleasant emotions. The power of not liking belongs to liking, without a relationship to emotion. The relationship of liking is to what you know in your heart; it's to what you love. That makes you all-weather love.

All-weather love is the beginning of the integration of your self. Your nervous system configures to what you know rather than what you want for your self. Your self turns to face what you really are. When you are in what you love, difficulty doesn't hinder you. It helps you reach even more deeply into what you love. A storm doesn't stop the growth of a tree. The tree directs its energy to the roots and the roots grow deeper.

Listening

WHAT MATTERS IS HOW DEARLY YOU
LISTEN WITHIN, THEN HOW MUCH YOU LET
YOURSELF SEE, AND FINALLY, HOW YOU
FOLLOW THROUGH

Questioner: You have said that eternity is a being. What is love?

John: Expression of eternity.

Questioner: What is that in relation to truth?

John: Truth is the stillness, and love is its movement.

Questioner: How do they become one?

John: They are one.

Questioner: How can movement and stillness be one?

John: Stillness moving. Stillness moving is true movement, quality movement. That's what makes the presence of a tree so lovely.

Questioner: I wanted to ask you about listening.

John: When you have more seeing than listening, it makes you oriented to experience. That opens up the loveliness of experience with a lack of stillness. It is listening within that is at the leading edge of stillness. With seeing there is already a coming out. In listening within, everything stops. With real listening within you can't be coming from anything that you can already see. In listening within you are able to know something that you cannot yet see. There is not yet an understanding of what you know. It is the listening within that connects you with such knowing, even though you cannot understand. As the attention of awareness is listening, knowing fills the heart and stillness leads to seeing. The eyes of the heart see what they have never seen before.

The listening is without the need to see. There is then an authoritative knowing, no longer limited by experience, but guided by real listening within. Let awareness distinguish itself from seeing so that it can listen. There is surrender in listening. There isn't necessarily surrender in seeing. No vastness of seeing matters if there is not the most delicate listening.

Seeing means that there has been virtue living in the heart. Without virtue living in the heart, all value is an assumed value. When virtue is living in the heart, living value permeates everything. Eternity is present. With seeing there is past credit, whereas listening requires present virtue. Seeing shows you the truth of what was. Real listening within shows you what newly, presently, is.

What matters is how dearly you listen within, then how much you let yourself see, and finally, how you follow through. You can get away with having excitement in seeing, but in real listening there is only stillness, being able to hear something within that you have never heard before. It is listening within that lets eternity come into form, which is virtue. Virtue in the heart is eternity in form. Without that, everything that you think you have, including seeing, is perishable.

Real listening enables you to see what
is imperishable, to live what is imperishable.
It is listening that lets you see and live what
is eternal. You cannot really listen within without
having love. Really listening within is the
beginning of love, a quieted willingness.

CHAPTER 3

Creating a New Self

As you surrender to what you know in your heart, there is more and more to realize. There are streams and levels that may imply a change in your life, or simply the invitation to give your heart to a slightly softer quality of being. Within the deeper levels of your self and your heart is your being, timeless yet human, universal yet individual. Our beings provide that whisper we have all known since we were children, that repeats in every quiet moment that there is something more.

When your honesty reaches to the core of your heart, through every belief or investment you hold, your being becomes available. Your being moves into the very structures of your self and your life, so that the whisper of a higher reality becomes the actual form of who you are in this life. It is a constant surrender through profound honesty and the manifestation of love in the structures of the world. Your eternal being becomes who you are on the earth.

Openness and softness of heart does answer your life. Your relationships are waiting to open along with your own heart. Your struggles settle as your heart settles. The condition of your heart determines the condition of your self, manifested in every part of your life. Even in awful circumstances, openness and softness of heart takes you home. Yet, in its immense value, openness and softness is not for your benefit. Access to your deeper levels is given to belief, pure and without condition. In return, your self and your person receive the influence of your being, an influence of most profound correction, with no regard for your personal beliefs or investments.

Everything tied to your life will be untied by the purpose of your being, reweaving form to suit what you know is deepest in you.

Authentic Availability

MAKE FULL EXPRESSION OF YOUR OWN
HEART IN YOUR SELF

If you're not coming from what you really are, your self is occupied with your identity. Your belief is given to what cannot sustain you. Who you are is closed to the deep. When you're being what you really are, your self is available; who you are is filled with what you are. Your heart comes into your self because your being is in your heart, your innermost becoming real in you. Regardless of anything that you're experiencing, return to your heart. Make full expression of your own heart in your self.

From Anger to Reasonableness

THE ENERGY IN ANGER IS A MISPLACED
RESOURCE. BE HEARTFULLY RATIONAL
INSTEAD OF BEING RIGHT

Stifled by another's unreason, you may feel justified in anger, but anger would only expose that you lack depth in your reasonableness. You value reason, but if you're pushed to a certain point, you give it up. In that, you give undue importance to yourself, and self-importance is provoked to anger. The energy in anger is a misplaced resource. Be heartfully rational instead of being right.

Be profoundly honest the moment you feel the first twinges of reaction. The anger begins with a micro-tightening in your heart. If you don't catch it there, it grows. You will take rightness over openness, being right instead of responsive. If you harden your heart to achieve something, even something that you perceive as right, you've abandoned a depth of meaning in you. If you succumb to anger, be open to see how you have misplaced meaning.

When you're angry there's a fire out of control in you, regardless of the rightness of your position, and you need to pull the fire alarm. Everything that's taking place in you ends, and everyone in you has to leave the building. When the fire is out, then everyone can come back into the building. When you come back in, you'll have perspective. Let the heating point be your last reminder to open and soften.

The energy that fuels negative emotion is your power to believe what is true. You are then whole in being. Your appreciation of reason turns into a love of reasonableness.

As the years pass, you will develop a character far more precious than all those opportunities to be right.

The more that you release the energy of negativity, the more your unintegrated self becomes your tender reminder to soften.

What is Love?

THE MOMENT THAT TRUTH MOVES, EVER SO SLIGHTLY, THERE IS LOVE

Real love is the most wonderful and life-giving energy in the universe. It cannot comprehend frustration. It cannot be provoked to be anything other than love. It is kindness and tenderness without thought, without willfulness. It does not self reflect. It does not consider itself. Pressure never changes it. Pressure only reveals its depth. Love flourishes in fire. When anything other than love is in the fire, it is something other than lovely. Fire is the grand revealer of what is love and what is not. The hotter the fire, the more love flows and shines.

Love has no inner dialogue; it doesn't need to think to be. It needs no thought, and yet it can most wonderfully express itself through thought. When love dies, when it returns to its own source, it does so without a sound. When love dies, it does not leave a trace. When truth is still, there is no love, there is nothing but truth. You cannot see it, you cannot find it, but the moment that truth moves, ever so slightly, there is love.

The movement of truth is love.
Love is the manifestation of truth,
and there is no other.

Containing Meaning

WHEN MEANING IS SAFE IN YOUR HEART,
MEANING GROWS IN YOU, AND YOU COME
INTO DEPTH OF CHARACTER

As you open, love and meaning flow into you. All this meaning is yours to beautifully contain in your heart. You simply know its goodness without spending it through your patterns. In the experience of meaning, whatever is unintegrated in your self grabs on, and it is easy to spend the meaning to benefit your experience. If you simply rest in it, the meaning enfolds you, and when you do express meaning, you don't express because you can, but because you know.

You come into a quiet power, the power in what you know is true, and regardless of how something burns in your self, you remain gentled and quieted. If you contain meaning, the power of your being comes into your self and fills, and is quietly, gently contained. With containment, you're able to fill with love, without any need to love someone. You will be a love-filled person without needing to show it. You will have a presence of love without needing to express it. The presence is what fundamentally communicates.

In the same way, when experience is low, remain in your heart, and your self will heal. Meaning fills your self and its power is safe in you, and others are safe with you. When your sensibilities are ever so slightly offended, you'll not roll your eyes, not on the outside and not on the inside. The offence goes in without any personal comment. And when someone hurts you, even slightly, you won't throw your eye. The hurt just simply and quietly goes in.

When you contain meaning in your heart, your being can also enter your self, just as the hurt enters, to be quietly contained. When meaning is safe in your heart, meaning grows in you, and you come into depth of character. It isn't a performance; it's rooted in the good ground of openness and softness of heart.

You need no reward in being what love is. When you are what love is, you're not needing its return. Love doesn't need to be answered. It just quietly and freely gives.

The Intelligence of Love

YOUR BEING MOVES WITH THE INTELLIGENCE OF LOVE. LOVE, AND YOU WILL KNOW THE PERFECTION OF YOUR BEING

Questioner: When I met with you in Tiruvannamalai, you spoke of love as a quiet river with many streams in it. You invited me to learn to discern within the streams and currents. I have been pondering the meaning of the stream, and when you mentioned the word "oneness," you brought my awareness there. Is that like calling on what you really are?

John: You, awareness, in response to what you know, are oneness. Your movement as oneness is love, moving through each of your energy centres without design or purpose as the infilling of your self by all of your being. In all of your interior, move freely as love.

Questioner: I love hearing this.

John: Within your being, there are no boundaries, like those that define your self. In your self, just as in your being, let love move freely.

Questioner: I'd like to hear that again, please.

John: As a person, you naturally relate to your energy centres, where frequencies of meaning, emotion, and levels of your being meet locations in your body. You relate to them through a system in your self of filters and boundaries. In your self, the relationship to the energy centres is by governing them based on attraction and aversion. You establish a comfort zone in which you open or close your energy centres depending on your experience of your self. There is no need to manage your energy centres from within your self. You, in response to what you know, are oneness. You are love moving through each of your energy centres without design or purpose, filling your self with all of your being. At its outside, each centre touches a different region of your self and, at the core, each energy centre reaches your being.

Energy centres are not to be gates of control in the self, but points of entrance for your being into your self. When you are unconditionally opening and softening, your energy centres open and your being moves in response to everything that addresses your self. You open to all that you awaken to. Your being is the purpose of your energy centres and your energy most deeply belongs to your being.

Questioner: Can I ask you to say what the being is?

John: Perfectly interconnected, dynamic structures of love. Perfect forms of what you really are. Your real multi-leveled body, a body of pure you, unrecognized by this world, is to be beautifully seated in your self. When you are unconditionally open and soft, your gates open and your being, moved by the truth, streams through in ownership of your self and your life. Your self, in all of its polarity, changes as if by magic. But the truth of it is as simple as resting. Rest and you are love.

Openness and softness is you, relaxed in what you know. You are moved in your being, one in the intelligence of love. It's the perfection of how you move through your energy gates, creatively manifesting your being in your self. Your being moves with the intelligence of love.

Questioner: A smile is coming to my face as you say that.

John: It's as simple as relaxing. You relax and you are love.

Questioner: What is the intelligence of love?

John: It's the perfection of how you move from within your being through your energy gates, creatively manifesting your being in your self. Love, and you will know its intelligence.

CHAPTER 4

True Parenting

Children are complete beings, but if you bring them into the world or under your wing, they become your precious responsibility, and the need to evolve multiplies. As your self forms to the condition of your heart, children form to you. They come to you for the quality of your being, living in your open heart. If you are true to what you know in your heart, your integrity is visible in everything you do, and children can rest in you.

It isn't your ideas and your words.
Your children are learning from what you are being.

Making Your Heart as a Womb

YOU CAN DEEPLY BE A PARENT WHEN
YOU'RE MORE RECEPTIVE THAN YOU CAN
COMPREHEND

Questioner: I've been trying to have a baby, and it's not happening and I wonder how to deal with that. It feels like it's taken everything from me.

John: It's taken everything from you because you're taking meaning from everything else and you're giving in to the desire of becoming pregnant. Let go of the need for a baby and remain profoundly honest in your heart, and therefore, your womb. If you're not honest to what is more profound than having a baby, how are you going to raise this baby? If your way of being matters more to you than becoming pregnant, that level of honesty will also be how you raise a baby.

In trying to become pregnant, you are separating from your own being, while inviting another being to come into your body and grow. In your invitation, you need to let go of your perceived needs and open your heart. Your heart needs to become like your womb. Then the tiniest little bit that you know the truth of in your heart will grow in your heart. If you take your self to heart, there's no room for your being in your heart.

The only way that you can deeply parent is for your heart to be like a womb, more receptive than you can comprehend. That begins before you have your baby, and it needs to flourish in all of your life. If you love openness and softness, you will make your heart just like your womb, whether you have a baby or not.

Forming Your Child by Clarity

CHILDREN ARE LEVELS AND LEVELS OF
ABILITY. AWAKENED TO THAT, THEY LOVE
TO BE REACHED

For you to live by what you know in your heart is for you to enter a much deeper level of parenting. You will be parenting your self and your nervous system. You will be parenting your own person. You'll be guiding your self according to your deeper knowledge instead of giving in to your self just because it begs for attention.

Your nervous system doesn't tell you the truth; it keeps you in touch with the condition of your own self. Your nervous system is designed for your self before it is reconfigured to what you know, reshaped by your heart. When you live in restedness, you move against your own inflamed nervous system. It hurts, but your nervous system begins to change and heal in response to your heart, and your children become an extension of your rested nervous system.

As you open, you will be growing up. With surrender to what you know in your heart, you will be conforming to your own being in the midst of a nervous system that is hardwired to your patterns. Your children will respond to your restedness. Just as your nervous system responds, and as you raise your children through your heart, you also raise your self. When you are being clear while your child is distressed, the child is reading you. The child sees your clarity and trusts you, and the two of you meet. The child's nervous system matches yours, and the child is free of frustration. The child realizes the love of learning and of change. They meet difficulty with ease. Difficulty enables them to realize what they are. Children are levels and levels of ability. Awakened to that, they love to be reached.

And you will not always manage. Opening your nervous system and raising your child will be temperamental, but instead of measuring your difficulties with your nervous system, measure your difficulties with your clarity, and love learning. Then when you shout, and you see the shock in their eyes, that's your cue to drop everything and hug them.

What your children most deeply want is you from the innermost outwards. They want all of you. They want to see all of you in the details. That makes it very inviting for them to be all that they really are with the details, within the little things. Your children love the little things.

The Responsibility of Raising a Child

WHEN TWO PARENTS ARE TOGETHER IN
DEARNESS, THE CHILD LEARNS TO REST
IN GOODNESS

A child is looking for a multi-leveled, multi-dimensional inner reality, and looking for it in you. If you are governed by what you actually know the truth of within, and manifesting that through clear use of mind, your child will attune to you and follow you deeper.

A child places a huge demand for authenticity on your relationship. When there's nothing unclear at play, no willfulness or manipulation, when everything is from a higher perspective, and two parents are together in dearness, the child learns to rest in goodness. But for the child to rest, the responsibility of parenting needs to land deeply in the parent. All your deeper levels are required of you. Nothing can compensate for that because your relationship with your own heart is the beginning of everything that matters.

Parenting means giving your child reality that he or she has never seen. Bring your child into levels within that he or she hasn't realized yet. Then when an issue flares, an open heart is the first little door that opens, and because of the depth that you have opened together, into that little door you both jump.

The bond between you is everything, built through profound honesty. The bond allows you and your child to meet. Allowing a child to come into your life, through you, is really the need to allow your being to come through you. The wide-open innocence of a child finds all the gaps in you, and rests wherever there is a bed of authenticity. When you bring a child into the world, the innocence of that being exacts your deepest and finest clarity. The beauty is that you will stumble, but where there is honesty, both you and your child are safe.

When your children are in a bad mood, it is because they miss you.

CHAPTER 5

True Relationship

Nothing requires your deeper resources like a relationship in which two are together for the highest reason, to manifest truth in the whole person, from the heart to the practical details. Your being is the profound nurturer of your relationship, and your relationship belongs solely to your being. The finest of what you know in your heart is brought out in relationship because there is the greatest capacity of love and the greatest need to lay down your investments. When everything that it means to be human is called up to meet another, the responsibility and the opportunity is immense. The responsibility is to surrender all you have for what you know in your heart. The opportunity is for everything in your life to be formed by love.

True relationship offers the most exquisite streams of deeper meaning, realized in the everyday.

Always Being Reached

IN REAL RELATIONSHIP, BOTH DIFFICULTY AND MEETING BRING YOU DEEPER

In meeting, there is unspoken agreement to reach and to be reached, allowing anything on the surface to rearrange according to goodness. Everything needs sorting out, but from the perspective of who you are meeting. Meeting means that the orientation in each is deeper than the selves of either.

In real relationship, there isn't room for a speck of needing to be right. In real relationship, there is always room for both to be reached. In real relationship, both difficulty and meeting bring you deeper. There isn't personal space. Neither of you needs to have the privacy of a corner. All of the space is available for meeting. You are together despite any difficulties, and giving your hearts is constant and practical. Meeting and reaching become the form of relationship. As relationship deepens there is giving and giving and giving. Giving is what meaning does.

In real relationship, when there is meeting, hearts grow bigger and selves grow up.

Connection to the Innermost

WHEN YOUR HEART OPENS, YOUR MIND AND BODY OPEN, AND YOUR BEING HAS YOUR RELATIONSHIP

Love between two is constantly testing the depth of your honesty; the interplay of personality reveals every little crack. The piercings of relationship invite you to return to your heart and allow love to express itself through everything, including the personality. To be what love is outside of the personality feels safer than being love through the personality. It is where love meets personality that the friction shows up. Any self-interest, when love moves through the personality, gets stuck, and you seem to lose your first love. Nothing is lost, but you, as awareness, have been bought. Release your investments, and you return to your first love. The finest of love is when it moves through the personality without getting stuck. Awareness becomes very fine, knowing how to move as love, through sensation, without being distracted by sensation.

When your heart opens, your mind and body open, and your being has your relationship. When you then touch someone, the sensation goes all the way to your innermost. It is the experience of your being, connecting with another with the slightest touch.

The experience of that is so complete that, if anything in you relates to want, you cease being what you know, and you'll try to do it again, just because you liked it. But if you remain true in what you know, then such an experience is no distraction. You distinguish between your experience and the truth you know within it. What you know is true is what you're in a body for, what you're in relationship for. That makes you and your relationship always new.

Let your deeper levels within be the connectivity in your relationship, where you speak and where you meet.

Feathering a Nest

BECOMING YOUR TRUE, SOFTENED POTENTIAL IN RESPONSE TO EACH OTHER

A softened masculine energy builds a nest. A softened feminine energy feathers the nest. When each is softened, the movements of energy see each other and respond. Each learns to become the very finest it sees in the other. An unintegrated masculine energy controls through force as an unintegrated feminine energy controls through manipulation. Building a nest is no longer using the power of each in order to protect and control. The power of each opens up, and a nest comes together, a space held and feathered for truth to have a home.

The energy of want within builds a nest also, but not the kind that love makes. The nest that love makes is built by grace. The nest holds something more wonderful than the individuals in the relationship. Through the pressures of life, two become their true softened potential in response to the other. A relationship starts out as being terribly good. If grace reigns, the relationship becomes only good. Grace builds and never takes. Each person, sees the very finest within the other being mastered by nothing else.

In the Light and Dark of Marriage

A RELATIONSHIP IS MEANT TO TAKE BOTH OF YOU INTO AWAKENING

Walking into the doors of marriage is like walking into a beam of light. It reflects the goodness of the bond. It is the flow of what you really are, together. That beam of light is the third being. It is the being of your relationship. And as nurturing and wonderful and rich as it is, it will be that awful as well because you enter the light with all your patterns. You walk with full agreement into the relationship between your beings. Will you remain in that agreement, after the doors have closed behind you and the light goes out?

A relationship is meant to take both of you into awakening. But if you are hanging onto your rights to be loved, to be needed, to be appreciated, you cover up the bond, and it is your patterns, not your hearts, that are in relationship. Be together for both of you to remain gentled and quieted and stilled, for your personal interests to lose their hold. Being gentled and quieted in the midst of the worst, you manifest the beauty of your interior.

The bond that is between the two of you is worth more than each of your minds. If you honour your thinking in the relationship, your relationship will be confined to your minds. The bond between the two will go underneath, unfelt, unrealized for everything it really is. The heart of the other is a living energy that you pour your heart into without expecting anything in return. That is the way to be in marriage, for each of you to honour that this is the ground in which you are to be buried. This is where your opinions and your ideals, your hopes and your dreams die, and what lives is the nectar of your bond.

Marriage is for what you are as a being. When you go into marriage only for that little bit that you know is true, and you abide in that for better or for worse, then what grows is meaning, and meaning provides your being.

A high level of relationship depends on each person completely belonging to goodness within.

Dearness

NESTING IN AN OPEN AND SOFT HEART,
DEARNESS SHARES SPACE WITH THE UTTERLY
PROFOUND

The beginning of real relationship is dearness. It is an essential energy that brings meaning to physical reality. Everything that thrives that is outside of dearness will pass away despite what you've invested in it. Dearness is so palpable, but so fine that your wants and needs can easily overshadow it.

Dearness is what meets in the midst of all disagreement. It is the nurture within your strengths and your weaknesses. It is the part that matters within everything that pulls at your attention. Dearness is always with you, so close that you are always either carrying it or stepping on it. You're able to deprive it and you're able to give it life. And then there are all of the deeper levels to you and existence, to which dearness is a door.

Dearness lives in an open and soft heart. It is so basic that every person knows it, but so tenderly profound, that it becomes as elusive as the deeper levels of your being.

Nesting in an open and soft heart, dearness shares space with the utterly profound. But when the most profound levels of awareness begin to enter the self through the heart, they are led by dearness.

CHAPTER 6

A Deeper Level of Sexuality

Sexuality is the most powerful form of human expression. We have no greater way of moving meaning, of manifesting love. The ways of sexuality in our world show how delicate this power is, registering hugely the slightest separation from what we know in our hearts. The full spectrum of human consciousness is available to sexual connection, and like the full spectrum of consciousness, the truth of sexuality begins with openness and softness of heart, and a profound honesty that lives for streams of realization.

Reformed by the being, sexuality is given back to a vast purity, often forgotten, but core to the purpose of sexuality, which is holy.

Giving Your Sexuality to Your Being

LOVE ISN'T A FEELING. LOVE IS HOW YOUR BEING MOVES

Questioner: You described a relationship based on what you know, but can't see, and don't understand. Can you explain this, John?

John: Take your relationship deeper than your selves, where it grows from what you know in your heart, where you aren't relating through likes and dislikes, but together in a love that comes from the deep. There, you don't first see each other, but purely know each other, and then you see each other, and then you come to understand each other. You forgive each other of the selves you have, and your selves no longer need to be a problem. This creates the environment within which your beings are together. Instead of remaining unseen between you, love is made physical. The levels of your being are made real in your selves, through your body.

Questioner: It's a dream come true.

John: Love isn't a feeling. Love is how your being moves. In your familiar self, you cannot see it at first. It comes into your self as you begin to move in the levels of your own being. Your introduction to that movement is the softening of your heart, where you and your wife meet in dearness. Because you are in a body, when you move by these levels, they become physical. Instead of being a body of your self, you are a body of your being. The flow of your being changes your self in this life. Love becomes seen in each of you and between you.

As you meet as beings, you don't relate by the sexual appetite of your conditioning. You relate through a deeper sexuality, your real capacity within your being to meet and commune. Real sexuality is streams of being, comprehended in your body. As you respond, you reconfigure. As you become even a little bit like your being, you find her everywhere in her body.

Questioner: How can I respond to her more?

John: Begin with dearness. Dearness in you finds her and, in any little way she moves as dearness, you read her and receive her. Sexuality isn't for your selves, but for your beings. Moving in deeper sexuality doesn't require maturity. It requires purity. Dearness brings you into purity.

Questioner: What is dearness?

John: Dearness is your heart reaching. It cannot occur without you being in what you know in your heart. From there, any movement toward each other is the simplest form of love. You are purely dear to each other, despite what selves you have, despite what conditioning and past you have. You come together in dearness, come together in response to each other. You'll know each other and you'll see each other. The effect of that on your selves is quiet wonderment, exquisite because it is pure. Begin in your heart and find the same in her. Begin in your heart, the two of you together and wonderfully inexperienced.

Your sexuality is integrated in your self, not by you doing something with it, but by you being completely in it while you are staid in your heart.

Deeply and Truly Human

YOUR HEART, WIDE OPEN, MAKES YOU
DEEPLY AND FULLY HUMAN

Being truly human has little to do with your self and everything to do with the opening of your heart. You are most deeply human when your heart is open and you are unconditionally at rest. Your sexuality is your engine in that movement, the engine of your humanness.

When you are not opening and softening in your heart in the midst of your sexuality, sexuality becomes the engine to self-orientation, an orientation around attraction and aversion. When you are in your heart in the movement of your sexuality, the energy of sexuality opens you into a depth of humanness.

When you are in your heart, seeing with those deeper eyes, your humanness moves into your patterned self. Kindness moves, a kindness free of any results. Authentic kindness moves. As it moves, your heart comprehends others. The deeper levels of your being move into the deeper levels of your body, making love physical in your self, in your conscious experience, accomplishing pure human love.

Your heart, wide open, holding only what it knows is true, makes you deeply and fully human. Your subconsciousness then has access into your conscious self, so that there's no longer a barrier between who you are and all of your interior. There is just all of you, knowing, loving, and seeing, a fully functional human being.

From within your heart, be attentive to any delicacies of your being, which move your sexuality from your heart into your being. From there, it comes back again, into your self, with an even deeper purity.

Making Love in Meaning

YOUR ENTRANCE INTO THE MEANING OF
SEXUALITY IS COMPLETELY DEPENDENT
ON TENDERNESS, BEING GENTLED AND
OPEN IN YOUR HEART

You can learn how to make love without having sex, making love purely in your connection. In conditioned sexuality there is a build up towards a peak of experience, but reaching that peak is like approaching a closed door, where the very meaning you were looking for, and seeing and gaining, is gone. When sexual energy resides in the heart, then as you reach a climax, you are brought into the very deep of everything you knew was available.

A sexual peak is meant to be a full and a complete entrance, an immersion into your innermost, but the intensity of meaning is what so easily distracts, leading you back into conditioned sexuality. The experience offers you the fullness of goodness, but when you reach the climax you wanted, the coarseness of your pursuit is exactly what distances you from the meaning. What you really want is the immersion into your innermost. Its truth is available in your rested heart, before sexual energy begins to even move.

When you are rested in your heart, exploring sexuality for the love of meaning and communion, you are able to meet the other, being-to-being. After the physical communion as beings, you have within your heart a deposit from what is beyond. As it grows within your heart, your mind slowly comprehends. Your entrance into the meaning of sexuality is completely dependent on tenderness, being gentled and open in your heart. As consciousness you can only go as high as you let tenderness descend. Everything there is truly good, and the way you entrust yourselves to each other is how you are outside of the bedroom. Being in your bond, you are making love all the time.

Your sexuality is able to move by streams of your own being. The fulfillment of your sexuality isn't in the physical. It is in your being moving within all of your sexuality.

Returning Sexuality to Your Being

THE ANSWER TO THE PRESSURE OF SEXUAL ENERGY IS REALIZATION

Your own sexuality is profoundly answered when your sexuality is returned to your being. When your sexuality moves, your being moves. For you to live that way is the complete transformation of your self. You would be giving all of the power to your heart, and giving your heart to your own being.

If your appetites are not mastered by your heart, then your appetites will rule you. Your appetites, in that way, are like children. If your appetites are out of control, the responsibility is yours. Your appetites are innocent. When your appetites are mastered by you being in your heart, then your self comes under the mastery of what

THE INTELLIGENCE OF LOVE

you know the truth of in your heart instead of you giving in to what you think and feel in your self.

If you are governed by the patterns of attraction or aversion, you either satisfy your appetites simply because you can, or you suppress them. If you're really in your power in the midst of your appetites, all of your power is governed by the quietest of what you know in your heart. The quietest power in you rules all of the strong powers in you. All the energy of your sexuality then moves inward and enriches your being, and your being moves into your self, where your honesty has created so much space.

If you reside in your heart, and listen quietly to what you know, your sexuality brings realization. The answer to the pressure of sexual energy is realization. When you open in the midst of your sexuality, you begin to realize its depth, and its depth moves just like your own being; it moves as love.

CHAPTER 7

Your Being in this World

The world is the collective self of all the people in it and, like our selves, is not the purpose for its own existence. The world does not need to change, just as the experience of our selves needs no amelioration. However, as the purpose of the human being awakens, the world responds and changes, just like our selves transform from the influence of our beings.

There is consciousness in everything. There is knowing in everything, and its purpose is to be given to the deepest meaning it knows. When we give our selves and lives to what we know in our hearts, we are available for our beings. The planet is available for us; the planet is waiting for our awakening. Its nature is inherently open and soft and true, reminding us how to be.

Our Nature in Waiting

NATURE ISN'T LOOKING TO BE SAVED;
IT IS LOOKING TO YOUR BEING

The nature around you is not relating to its own life, but to your being. The relationship is so clean that you love it without even thinking. Any concern for the state of nature is really your own issue, as nature has no concern for itself. The essence of a tree is there whether the tree is living or not, just as when you die, you still are. Now you see through the density of form, making your personal experience of more apparent value than your being, and the planet of more apparent meaning than the being of this planet. Nature reaches the depths of you that go beyond this life because nature speaks to your being.

If someone serves you superficially, without seeing you, you are missed. At your core, you would rather be known and seen than served. Nature isn't looking to be saved; it is looking to your being, as the being of the earth responds to our awakening.

When you have your own being, you have it all. When you have everything in life, separate from your being, what you have amounts to nothing. Life isn't as we perceive it to be. Life is as we know it in our beings, where the meaning of life becomes available, tangible, and practical. When our belief is given to what we know in our hearts, our beings begin to stream, and with the presence of nature that is already open, we awaken.

When you are less than what your self is, that makes you more than the sum of all of your experiences, enabling you to guide your self into goodness. The world around you can then follow the less, on the way to the greater.

A Full Spectrum of Consciousness

NATURE AWAKENS WHEN WE GROW UP, NOT JUST AS HUMANS, BUT AS CLEAN BEINGS

The typical human has a full spectrum of consciousness. With a full spectrum of consciousness, we are able to be other than our beings, derived from the true ability to know ourselves and to be everything that we really are.

Nature, as a being, has a narrower spectrum of consciousness, relating as love and merging with its likeness in us. But simply being its own essence, nature is unable to be other, and so cannot consciously be. So, while nature and humanity are connected on the level of the being, we experience separation. That is why the beauty of nature fulfils and yet creates longing. We long to merge fully with the beauty we sense.

When we grow up, not just as humans, but as clean beings, nature responds, and we merge with nature. Consciousness and beauty integrate. The awakening of nature depends on us being what we truly are. Until then, nature is simply itself. It knows itself when we know ourselves. Then nature's purity gains awareness and our awareness gains purity.

Being the Healing

IN YOUR HEART, EVERYTHING CAN
BE INTEGRATED

Questioner: I am concerned about the world, climate change, the environment. How can I be in it all?

John: Be in the world as you know to be in your self, one with what you know in your heart. When the deeper is in your self, it draws up your conditioning so that, in your heart, everything can be integrated. If you haven't really integrated your self, when you address the world you won't be heard. To be heard in this world there needs to be the continuity of what you really are, unbroken throughout all of you. Without that integrity, what you say won't have the appeal of the deep.

The effort to heal the planet distracts, unless the healing comes from the deep. If out of fear you address this world, you will be using the condition of this world to release what is only a tension in your self. The world is like you; it needs no preoccupation with itself. What you can be in the midst of it all is the tiniest bit you know is true in your heart. How can this world be shaped by what you know when your own self isn't yet shaped by what you know in your heart?

We don't truly change because of ideals; we change because we awaken to what we know matters most, and bring that into our hearts. The meaning of change is not to make our lives more comfortable, but in recognition of what is true, and deeper, and lovelier than what we knew before.

*When you are on your deathbed, and you look
back into your life, it won't matter to you what
you have done with your life. What will matter
to you is what you have done in all of your
life with your heart.*

Dearly in this World

YOUR WHOLE LIFE IS REALLY ONLY ABOUT
THAT DEAR PLACE IN YOU WHERE YOU
KNOW YOU'VE REALIZED, YOU LOVE,
AND YOU ARE REACHED

Questioner: What I see here is so big and beautiful. Why do I turn my back on what I love?
John: That is all secondary to your response to what you love.

Questioner: I respond at times, but not always.
John: As long as you are even just a little bit softer than your self, you're fine. However you're thrown in your self, what you love, and how that reaches you, is constant.

Your whole life is really only about that dear place in you where you know you've realized, you love, and you are reached.

Questioner: Mmmm, yes. Is it possible to be in touch with that more often and bring that into my daily life?

John: The part of you that is aglow with real knowledge and love bears no complaint to the parts that have not yet come to light.

Questioner: That's the beauty. I know that, but...

John: While you are crunching and grinding, your heart is melting.

Questioner: Yes...yes...yes. And I put my awareness there...

John: Just quietly in your heart.

For more information visit:
www.johnderuiter.com